THE GREAT EXCHANGE

WHAT HAPPENED IN THE GARDEN OF EDEN

LAURA HAYWOOD-MAINS

WESTBOW
PRESS®
A DIVISION OF THOMAS NELSON
& ZONDERVAN

WestBow Press books may be ordered through booksellers or by contacting:

WestBow Press
A Division of Thomas Nelson & Zondervan
1663 Liberty Drive
Bloomington, IN 47403
www.westbowpress.com
844-714-3454

ISBN: 978-1-6642-4163-3 (sc)
ISBN: 978-1-6642-4164-0 (e)

Library of Congress Control Number: 2021915263

Print information available on the last page.

WestBow Press rev. date: 09/02/2021

CONTENTS

DEDICATION

I would like to share my gratitude to my wonderful husband, Rollin, and for all his support. Rollin, you have been by my side through a lot of tough times over the past eleven years. You have supported me and allowed me to grow as a woman of God and answer the call on my life for ministry. I cannot express the thankfulness I have in my heart for that and you; it means everything to me.

I also want to thank my best friend and close-as-a-sister Cintry Heinrich for all your support through many phone calls and all your prayers.

My children, grandchildren, and my brother and his family, you are all the heartbeats of my life. I love you all and thank you. I pray and know the Lord will continually bless you all the days of your lives.

PREFACE

This book is the first book I wrote but my second book to publish. Time has a way of taking important matters and turning them into insignificant matters. It has taken me twelve years to publish this book. But with that, I really want to convey one very important thing from this experience. I wrote this book supernaturally. I never thought of writing, or even wanted to write before this book. I heard the Lord say to my spirit back in 2009, when my first husband, Allan, was ill, to get up and start writing a book. I said, "OK," and off I went to my laptop. Once I started writing, my fingers did not stop. Thus, here I present to you my first book written supernaturally within a few days led by the power of the Holy Spirit. When the Lord asks you to do something, I strongly encourage you to just say, "Yes." Now, through Him to you, here is my book: enjoy!

INTRODUCTION

Satan is a thief. He comes to steal, kill, and destroy. I believe his attacks are strategic. John 10:10 says, "The thief cometh not, but for to steal, and to kill, and to destroy."

When Satan attacks our lives, he enters through the gates of our minds. The mind is the door to your life, and once he finds a way in, he can fulfill his plan on earth.

So can Satan use our lives to fulfill his evil purpose? Let us look at Simon Barjona, a disciple of Jesus, as an example:

> Jesus asked his disciples, "But whom say ye that I am?"
>
> And Peter answered, "Thou art the Christ, the Son of the living God."
>
> Jesus then replied, "Blessed art thou, Simon Barjona: for flesh and blood hath not revealed it unto thee, but my Father which is in heaven.
>
> And I say unto thee, that thou art Peter, and upon this rock I will build my church; and the gates of hell shall not prevail against it." (Matthew 16:15–18)

In this encounter, Jesus was saying that Peter had been given a divine revelation about his identity.

When the Holy Spirit reveals His Word to you, it passes through the natural realm and enters the spirit. In this case, the natural realm is the mind. The revelation of God cannot be stopped. Even the gates—the mind—of hell cannot stop it.

Can you imagine how good Peter must have felt? The Lord Himself praised him and called him blessed. I am sure Peter's confidence went up a few notches, so much that he allowed himself to get too opinionated.

Matthew 16:21–23 read,

> From that time forth began Jesus to shew unto his disciples, how that he must go unto Jerusalem, and suffer many things of the elders and chief priests and scribes, and be killed, and be raised again the third day. Then Peter took him and began to rebuke him, saying, "be it far from thee, Lord: this shall not be unto thee." But Jesus turned and said unto Peter, "Get thee behind me Satan; thou are an offence unto me: for thou savourest not the things that be of God, but those be of men."

Peter must have been embarrassed. So you see, the Holy Spirit gave Peter revelation, and then Satan countered with his plan. One can be used in this earth by the Lord and yes, also by our enemy. It is your choice. You always have a choice.

In the following chapters, we explore how to distinguish who is speaking to you. God wants you to know His voice so you can fellowship with Him daily and be His witness in the world. He wants to equip you with authority and wisdom for your life as He leads and guides you.

1

DOMINION

GOD CREATED ADAM and Eve. He was with them, loving them and walking with them. All that God created was given to man so that he would have dominion over the earth and power over his destiny.

Genesis 1:28 says:

> And God blessed them and God said unto them, be fruitful, and multiply, and replenish the earth, and subdue it: and have every living thing that moveth upon the earth.

God gave man life, protection, health, and prosperity. He gave him love—all of Himself for all of him. Everything He created He entrusted to His friend Adam to steward and multiply. He withheld no good thing from Adam and Eve. He fellowshipped with them daily, and communion was their seal. Humankind was His friend.

James 2:23 says, "Abraham believed God, and it was imputed unto him for righteousness: and he was called the Friend of God." That was His plan. However, there was another creature watching this great relationship develop. He, too, had been at the Father's side at one time; he had been blessed beyond measure. He was beautiful beyond description and endowed with power from the Most High.

Ezekiel 28:13 says:

> Thou hast been in Eden the garden of God; every precious stone [was] thy covering, the Sardis, topaz, and the diamond, the beryl, the onyx, and the jasper, the sapphire, the emerald, and the carbuncle, and gold: the workmanship of thy tabrets and of thy pipes was prepared in thee in the day that thou wast created.

His future was grand and secure, filled with the love of God Almighty. But as time passed, he decided that it was no longer enough to glorify God; he wanted more. He wanted to *be* God, so he rose against his future of divine purpose. He fought with God's angel, Michael, and lost. His name was Lucifer.

"How art thou fallen from heaven, O Lucifer, son of the morning! How art thou cut down to the ground, which didst weaken the nations!" the prophet Isaiah wrote of him. "For thou hast said in thine heart, I will ascend into heaven, I will exalt my throne above the stars of God: I will sit also upon the mount of the congregation, in the sides of the north: I will ascend above the heights of the clouds; I will be like the most High. Yet thou shalt be brought down to hell, to the sides of the pit" (Isaiah 14:12–15).

And in Revelation 12:3, 7–9, John wrote:

> And there appeared another wonder in heaven; and behold a great red dragon, having seven heads and ten horns, and seven crowns upon his heads … and there was war in heaven: Michael and his angels fought against the dragon; and the dragon fought and his angels, And prevailed not; neither was their place found anymore in heaven. In addition, he which deceived the whole world: he was cast out into the earth, and his angels were cast with him.

Satan watched God make man in His image. He saw Him give this new creature dominion over a glorious earth. Satan gnashed in envy, dripped with disdain, and thought about what he could do to get in man's place. If not in God's place, then he would be the god of this world. He would separate man from his dominion and reign in his place.

He thought out his plan carefully. After all, time was all he had. He was cast out of heaven with nothing to live for, cursed by God, and lost forever! So he showed up in the Garden of Eden and plotted the separation of God and Adam.

How did he separate them? Through the gate of man's mind.

God gave Adam a command (Genesis 2:16–17):

> And the Lord God commanded the man, saying, "Of every tree of the garden thou mayest freely eat: But of the tree of the knowledge of good and evil, thou shalt not eat of it: for in the day that thou eatest thereof thou shalt surely die."

According to the account in Genesis 3:1, "And he said unto the woman, 'Yea, hath God said, ye shall not eat of every tree of the garden?'"

Satan came to Eve and asked her a question; he challenged what God had commanded. He whispered into her thoughts, and Genesis 3:2 says, "And the woman said ..." Maybe she answered aloud, or perhaps she answered within her thoughts. The point is that Eve listened to the serpent, answered, and then made a decision that changed the course of human destiny.

Genesis 3:6 says, "And the woman saw ... and did eat." Yeah, it was a bad choice, wasn't it? *Wikipedia* defines "decision" as, "Something that somebody chooses or makes up his or her mind about, after considering it and other possible choices."

God had given Adam and Eve everything, but Satan came and suggested that there was more—that God was withholding things from them. He told them there was another way to get those things. So Eve considered her options. Sounds just like us, doesn't it?

Satan used the same lie that led to his own demise to bring humans down with him. He wanted to believe that God was holding back from him, and that is precisely the message he whispered into Eve's ear to see if she would listen. And she did! Why? Because she talked herself into believing that God *was* holding back, and she believed there was a better way.

Isn't that Satan's master plan? Think about it: So many people choose not to follow Jesus because they believe that serving God would not be as gratifying as their lives apart from Him. This encounter between Eve and the serpent is precisely where that false notion was born. People assume that if they turn their lives over to God, He will limit their potential and hold them back from the life they can make for themselves. Satan devised this plan so that humankind would not receive his full blessing on this earth or walk in the dominion that was given to us.

The great exchange took place in the garden that day. Adam and Eve traded God's power, life, and favor for fear, death, and the curse. Second Timothy 2:7 says, "For God hath not given us the spirit of fear; but of power, and of love and of a sound mind."

In the devastation wrought by the serpent's lie, God's son and daughter remained on the earth with all the resources He had provided, but their spirits had disconnected from the source of life, the tree of life, God. And eventually, their bodies died. According to Genesis 2:17, "But of the tree of the knowledge of good and evil, thou shalt not eat of it: for in the day that thou eatest thereof thou shalt surely die."

Henceforth, humans walked the earth alone without God. Satan had won. Entering through the gate of the mind, he succeeded in causing divine division. Adam and Eve could no longer commune with God. They lost their authority in the world and over their destiny. In this deception, humans gave it all away. Now they were lost, and as Satan took his place as god of this world, man was on the sidelines, looking in.

Second Corinthians 4:4 says, "In whom the god of this world hath blinded the minds of them." Adam gave up his birthright. his blessing. Handing dominion over to Satan, man put on fear as his clothing. Envy was his food. Power was something to fight for. Thus murder was conceived, brother against brother. Why? For destiny!

Genesis 4:8 says, "And Cain talked with Abel his brother: and it came to pass, when they were in the field, that Cain rose up against Abel his brother, and slew him."

The very power they were given freely by their Lord they are now fighting for!

2

THE DOOR

ADAM AND EVE were devastated! They had given everything away. Their eyes were opened, and they knew that Satan deceived Eve, and there was nothing they could do. They could not bear to face God for their grave mistake, so they ran and hid from their Lord.

Genesis 3:8 says, "And the Lord God called unto Adam, and said, "Where art thou?" Adam answered, "I heard thy voice in the garden, and I was afraid, because I was naked; and I hid myself."

Fellowship was now broken; they were no longer in one accord with God. Adam was lost and looking for a way back to his God. God was missing his friend Adam, and He was already putting His plan of action in order to bring the relationship back into harmony.

Thus came His Son, Jesus!

But time was going to be between both of them for a while before the relationship could be restored. Time almost became a curse for Adam and God. Like a romance between a man and a woman, the time apart broke both their hearts. God sent Jesus to take back what Satan stole from God and Adam. Through His death, Christ restored to us a way and a relationship with our heavenly Father, God. And in John 10:7, He says, "Verily, Verily, I say unto you, I am the door of the sheep."

John 14:6 says, "Jesus saith unto him, I am the way, the truth and the life: no man cometh unto the Father, but by me."

He is the door, the way back into God's presence. It is salvation, and in this transaction you receive Jesus into your heart as your Savior, and you receive eternal life. He restored our divine connection and gave us a home in heaven even while we live on earth; it's called the kingdom of God.

"I am the vine, ye are the branches," Jesus states in John 15:5. "He that abideth in me, and I in him, the same bringeth forth much fruit: for without me ye can do nothing."

He gave us back the garden—the blessing recorded in Deuteronomy 7—the life of God in us. All that was given to man in the beginning was now being handed back to him. A second chance! Jesus gave all of Himself for all of you. He took the keys of death and hell from Satan and said, "You now have power over your destiny."

Matthew 28:18 says that "All power is given unto me in heaven and in earth."

Mark 16:15–18 says,

> And he said unto them, Go ye into all the world, and preach the gospel to every creature. He that believeth and is baptized shall be saved; but he that believeth not shall be damned. And these signs shall follow them that believe; In my name shall they cast out devils; they shall speak with new tongues; They shall take up serpents; and if they drink any deadly thing, it shall not hurt them; they shall lay hands on the sick, and they shall recover.

Once again God has a relationship with humankind. Glory be to God! According to Colossians 1:26–27, "the mystery which hath been hid from ages and from generations, but now is made manifest to God's saints: to whom God would make known what is the riches of the glory of this mystery among the Gentiles; which is Christ in you, the hope of glory."

God hid the mystery for ages, which was that he was sending Jesus as the "doorway," so we could come back into His presence. He planted Jesus in the womb of Mary and hid Him from Satan until the day Jesus was led to his cousin John the Baptist. He had to be baptized to start His ministry. It was at that time and place that God revealed in heaven and earth that Jesus was His Son!

Matthew 3:17 says, "And lo a voice from heaven, saying, This is my beloved Son, in whom I am well pleased."

Since that day, He made it known that we can boldly come to the Father and walk and talk with him, like in the Garden of Eden. We read in Hebrews 4:16, "Let us therefore come boldly into the throne of grace."

That was the whole purpose of sending Jesus for you, so you can come boldly to Him daily, receiving your sonship and all that belonged to Adam is again yours. Not begging, not in shame, boldly as in a relationship. He wants you; He loves you. Go to Him, and dare to be in an intimate relationship with your Creator.

The only thing stopping you is you! Your own vain thoughts of, *I can't*, and, *I'm not worthy*. That is an insult to the One who gave you the gift—Jesus—so you can, and now you say no! Or are they your own vain thoughts? We explore that in the following chapter.

2

THOUGHTS

MAN IS A spirit that lives in a body that has a soul. It is made up of our minds, wills, and emotions. The entrance God uses in our lives is through one's heart when you receive Jesus as your personal Savior. And Satan's way into your life on the earth is always your mind.

> I pray God your whole spirit and soul and body be preserved blameless unto the coming of our Lord Jesus Christ. Faithful is he that calleth you who also will do it. (1 Thessalonians 5:23)

Satan still has residence here on earth for a limited time. And while he is here, he seeks your life and all that you have.

Why does he have residence for a limited time? Because he became the "god of this world" (2 Corinthians 4:4), when Adam and Eve ate from the tree in the Garden of Eden. Jesus defeated him on the cross through His death, and Satan was given eternal damnation. But it won't begin until Jesus comes back to redeem His church. Satan will reside on the earth until that day, the final day.

> And there was war in heaven: Michael and his angels fought against the dragon; and the dragon fought and his angels,
>
> And prevailed not; neither was their place found any more in heaven.
>
> And the great dragon was cast out, that old serpent, called the Devil, and Satan, which deceiveth the whole world: he was cast out into the earth, and his angels were cast out with him.
>
> And I heard a loud voice saying in heaven, Now is come salvation, and strength, and the kingdom of our God, and the power of his Christ: for the accuser of our brethren is cast down, which accused them before our God day and night.
>
> And they overcame him by the blood of the Lamb, and by the word of their testimony; and they loved not their lives unto the death.

Therefore rejoice, ye heavens, and ye that dwell in them. Woe to the inhabiters of the earth and of the sea! for the devil is come down unto you, having great wrath, because he knoweth that he hath but a short time. (Revelation 11:7–12)

John 10:10 says, "The thief cometh not, but for to steal, and to kill, and to destroy." Satan's master plan has never changed, and he will work through your mind to attempt to sow seeds, lies, that will subvert God's truth. His purpose is to fill you with the works of the flesh, "which are these; Adultery, fornication, uncleanness, lasciviousness, idolatry, witchcraft, hatred, variance, emulations, wrath, strife, seditions, heresies, envying, murders, drunkenness, reveling" (Galatians 5:19–20).

You may think that your everyday thought life is just that, but it is not so! Your thinking stems either from God's truth or Satan's lies.

Second Corinthians 4:4 says, "In whom the god (Satan) of this world hath blinded the minds of them which believe not, lest the light of the glorious gospel of Christ, who is the image of God, should shine unto them." This is what he is good at—blinding the minds—and he is using your mind against you.

Because of the fall of humankind, we have two connections: the mind of our flesh, which is connected to the sensual natural realm, and our spirit man, which is connected to the Spirit of God. The Word says, "For the flesh lusteth against the Spirit, ye and the Spirit against the flesh: and these are contrary the one to the other" (Galatians 5:17). The battle is the mind of the flesh fighting the renewed mind of God.

We are three parts, body, soul, and spirit. As emotional beings, our states of mind also determine how we feel and the perspective we have. Proverbs 23:7 says, "For as he thinketh in his heart, so is he."

We believe that because we have grown with thoughts, perspectives, and emotions, they are ours; we are their owners. But remember, your mind is the gate that leads into your life; it always has been. You must learn and discern the enemy's tactics by keeping your mind renewed. Your mind must be renewed *daily* with God's Word to keep it in a powerful, healthy state, so you can follow him with your spirit and fulfill His plan for your life. Romans 12:2 says, "And be not conformed to this world: but be ye transformed by the renewing of your mind, that ye may prove what is that good, and acceptable, and perfect will of God."

First Corinthians 2:16 says, "But we have the mind of Christ." We can only obtain this through meditation in His Word. Renewing your mind daily with God's Word and promises is like eating food daily. You must eat every day. Why? Because your body needs the calories for fuel to burn and to carry your physical being. Like that, your mind must feed on the Word of God daily too. It will use up the day's supply if you don't. That's why Matthew 6:11 says, "Give us this day our daily bread." He is talking about the Word of God, daily.

You must meditate daily on His Word to be powerful, strong, and filled with patience to obtain His precious promises. It will not happen any other way. That is why the Word of God tells us, "And now, dear brothers and sisters, one final thing. Fix your thoughts on what is true, and honorable, and right, and pure, and lovely, and admirable. Think about things that are excellent and worthy of praise" (Philippians 4:8 NLT).

This is food for your body, soul, and spirit.

Renewing your mind with the Word of God daily will fill you with the fruit of the Spirit, which is, "love, joy, peace, longsuffering, gentleness, goodness, faith, meekness, temperance" (Galatians 5:22–23).

This is life, healing, and health.

You cannot memorize the Word of God and expect to be strong in the Lord. The Word strengthens you daily when you open your Bible and read it with your eyes and read it out loud so you can hear it.

Proverbs 4:20-22 says, "My son, attend to my words; incline *thine ear* unto my sayings. Let them not depart from thine *eyes*; keep them in the midst of thine heart. For they are *life* unto those that find them, and health to all their flesh" (emphasis added).

What you see and hear become your thoughts, will form words, and will become your conversation about what you believe and have confidence in. Then you can walk strong, confident, and powerful, led by the Spirit of God, and having the mind of Christ!

3

SEED

IF YE HAD faith as a grain of mustard seed, Ye might say unto this sycamine tree, be thou plucked up by the root, and be thou planted in the sea; and it should obey you. (Luke 17:6)

In this verse Jesus is saying that the seed is what you need for faith to grow. This principle is obviously reflected in the natural order: A tomato seed is needed in order to produce a tomato plant, and so on. You would never put a tomato seed in the garage, go into the house, and expect to come back to a garden. You take the seed, plant it in the ground, water it, protect it, and then it grows and produces more than you planted.

This process is so ingrained within us that we think nothing of it. That's just the way it works. But Jesus is teaching us that our *words* are seeds. Whatever we speak, we sow. It is a system, and once it's in motion, it will have its own momentum.

If healing is the plant you want to grow in your personal garden, then plant scriptures of healing from God's Word, and speak the scriptures over your body and care for and protect that seed until it bears the fruit. In this case, the manifestation of healing.

Such is the system of receiving from the kingdom of God perfectly displayed in earth. Satan knows the power of a seed well cared for, which is why he wants to manipulate your thoughts to control your words!

James 3:1–6 says,

> For in many things we offend all. If any man offend not in word, the same is a perfect (mature) man, and able also to bridle the whole body. Behold also the ships, which though they be so great, and are driven of fierce winds, yet are they turned about with a very small helm, whithersoever the governor listeth. Even so the tongue is a little member, and boasteth great things. Behold, how great a matter a little fire kindleth! And the tongue is a fire, a world of iniquity: so is the tongue among our members, that it defileth the whole body, and setteth on fire the course of nature: and it is set of fire of hell.

Our thoughts become beliefs, and our beliefs become words that are embedded in our hearts, the very core of our beings. Your words reveal what you have confidence in. Whether based in truth or founded on lies, our beliefs become words that we sow into our own lives and the lives of those around us. Our thoughts will come out of our mouths and reveal the things we trust.

Satan twists God's creation and order. Over and over again he plants the idea that God's blessings will limit the human experience. But Satan's twisted ways are based in fear and bring on the curse of sickness, poverty, and death. If he can get his thoughts into your mind and mouth, they will become your demise. He seeks every opportunity to use you against you. Once he sets this in motion, Satan can leave and work on his next victim because it will have its own momentum as James talked about. And your momentum will be headed to the fulfillment of all that is negative.

The thoughts I am talking about can be about you, your spouse, and your children. They can be about your job, money, health, and everything else that affects your life. A lie can be so intertwined within your thinking that you cannot distinguish it. But if a thought is at all contrary to the promises of God, then it is from Satan. God's Word is life, and life means all that is good! This is the very place where the serpent tricked Eve.

In the beginning, your body, soul, and spirit were created in accordance with the Spirit of God. You were one with Him, and there was no division within you as there is now. Your mind, will, and emotions were one pure creation that perfectly reflected your Father's likeness. Can you imagine that? A life of peace and unity with God. It is this state of mind that the Bible describes as God's perfect will for humankind: "And be not conformed to this world: but be ye transformed by the renewing of your mind, that ye may prove what is that good and acceptable, and perfect will of God" (Romans 12:2.

But under the curse, a war is being waged within your own body. Romans 7:23–24 tells us, "But I see another law in my members, warring against the law of my mind, and bringing me into captivity to the law of sin which is in my members."

> Out of the same mouth proceedth blessing and cursing. My brethren, these things ought not so to be. Doth a fountain send forth at the same place sweet water and bitter? Can the fig tree, my brethren, bear olive berries? Either a vine, figs? so can no fountain both yield salt water and fresh. Who is a wise man and endued with knowledge among you? Let his shew out of a good conversation his works with meekness of wisdom. (James 3:10–13)

A good conversation—meaning speaking maturely—allows you to navigate your life with the tongue of blessing. If this were not possible, why would the Lord tell us to do it? It is possible, obtainable, and the only way. You must decide to live this way. It takes time to become mature, but it will happen, and you will see your life unfold in the direction you really want it to go. Your future is right under your nose.

Plead Your Case

You cannot trust your thoughts or emotions unless they line up with the Word of God. Satan perverts all that God has created and uses it against us. He uses your emotions against you and builds a case that would deny you your destiny. But God seeks to plant His Word in your spirit to build a case for an eternal life of love and joy in Him.

The prophet Isaiah recorded God's words to fallen humanity: "I, even

I, am he that blotted out thy transgressions for mine own sake, and will not remember thy sins. Put me in remembrance; let us plead together: declare thou, that thou mayest be justified" (Isaiah 43:25–26).

God will plead your case with you so that you will be justified!

In the court of all creation, God is leading us to come to Him in prayer with His Word so He can defend us. That's why He sent Jesus, our intercessor between humans and God on earth.

Hebrews 2: 9 says, "But we see Jesus, who was made a little lower than the angels for the suffering of death, crowned with glory and honor; that he by the grace of God should taste death for every man."

Jesus took on the seed of Abraham: "For verily he took not on him the nature of angels; but he took on him the seed of Abraham" (Hebrew 2:16). He did this so he could become our high priest. "Wherefore in all things it behoved him to be made like unto his brethren, that he might be a merciful and faithful high priest in things pertaining to God, to make reconciliation for the sins of the people" (Hebrews 2:17).

He is still our intercessor in heaven. In Hebrew 4:14, the Word tells us, "Seeing then that we have a great priest who has passed through the heavens, Jesus, the Son of God, let us hold fast our profession." In other words, we must hold firmly on to what we believe.

Why would God send Jesus on behalf of us and then have Him return to heaven and actively act as our high priest? The answer is because He loves us so much, and He is trying to get you back into the place of coming to Him and asking Him for anything you need. He set up a high priest to intercede for his Adam, which is man, the human being as a whole. Again, that is why he declares in Hebrews 4:16, "Let us therefore come boldly unto the throne of grace, that we may obtain mercy, and find grace to help in time of need.

God sent Jesus as our sacrifice and our active high priest to fight for us day and night because the accuser, Satan, has lied to us and said we cannot come to God and ask anything for ourselves or anyone. And if you do, God will slap you upside the head and tell you to leave because you have misbehaved. That is the lie Satan has used to blind the minds of humankind. But in actuality, Revelation 13:10 says this: "And I heard a loud voice saying in heaven, Now is come salvation, and strength, and the kingdom of God, and the power of his Christ: For the *accuser* of our brethren is cast down, which accused them before our God day and night" (emphasis mine).

Your accuser is Satan, and his trick is to accuse you through your own mind. Convinced of your own fate, he seeks to so diminish your confidence in the Lord that you are reduced to a powerless existence. John said it this way: "Beloved, if our heart condemn us not, then have we confidence toward God" (1 John 3:21).

Satan knows that if your do not have confidence in God, you will not call on the Lord. Or you may go to the Lord, but your confidence is so low you walk away, not believing He will answer your prayer requests.

We must settle the issue with God. He is a being that cannot lie as, Hebrews 6:18 states, and begin to allow your mind to be saturated with the truth. That by two immutable things, in which it was impossible for God to lie, we might have strong consolation who have fled for refuge to lay hold upon the hope set before us (Hebrews 6:18).

4

EMOTIONS

MIRIAM WEBSTER DICTIONARY Online defines "emotion" as, "an act, process, or instance of changing place, movement … An impulse or inclination of the mind or will … to move." In short, the word "emotion" means "motion!"

We humans are emotional to the core. Therefore, we cannot trust our thoughts because they frequently move (fluctuate, change). That is why God's Word says:

> I have set the Lord always before me: because He is at my right hand, I shall not be moved. (Psalm 16:8)

> Those who trust in the Lord are as Mount Zion, which cannot be moved but abides forever. (Psalm 125:1)

> [F]or the king trusted in the Lord, and through the mercy of the most high, he shall not be moved. (Psalm 20:7)

> Cast thy burden upon the Lord, and He shall sustain thee: He shall never suffer the righteous to be moved. (Psalm 55:22)

I have set the Lord continually before me; Because He is at my right hand, I will not be shaken. (Psalm 16:8)

He only is my rock and my salvation; he is my defense' I shall not be greatly moved. (Psalm 62:2)

He will not suffer thy foot to be moved: he that keepeth thee will not slumber. (Psalm 121:3)

He only is my rock and my salvation; he is my defense; I shall not be greatly moved. (Psalm 62:6)

A man shall not be established by wickedness: but the root of the righteous shall not be moved. (Proverbs 12:3)

God gave us His Word so that we can use it. He knows that we cannot discern our enemy's lies on our own. We need His truth in order to succeed, and He knows how to bring us through every problem. He wants us to plant His Word in our hearts so that it will become our flesh.

Truth defeats the devil in every area of your life. If your thoughts do not line up with God's promises, then Satan is whispering his way into your life. It is that black and white. According to Genesis 3:1, "Now the serpent was more *subtle* than any beast of the field which the Lord God had made" (emphasis mine).

Eve was tricked in her thoughts and emotions just as you are daily. However, if you stay close to the Holy Spirit through God's Word, you will recognize these tactics because they will contradict God's love and grace.

Keep His Word before you day and night, and you will not be moved by your emotions. Sure, you will feel the emotions, but you will be in control as you submit them through God. Then you will not allow yourself to act on them. You will act on the Word, and, therefore, you shall not be moved.

It is a fact that this will keep you in a strong position through any battle in life. Your demeanor will change, and you will say aloud, "My emotions are not in charge here. The Word of God is my stance!"

5

TRUST

FRET NOT THYSELF because of evildoers, neither be thou envious against the workers of iniquity.

For they shall soon be cut down like the grass, and wither as the green herb.

Trust in the Lord, and do good; so shalt thou dwell in the land, and verily thou shalt be fed.

Delight thyself also in the Lord; and he shall give thee the desires of thine heart.

Commit thy way unto the Lord; trust also in him; and he shall bring it to pass.

And he shall bring forth thy judgment as the noonday.

Rest in the Lord, and wait patiently for him: fret not thyself because of him who prospereth in his way, because of the man who bringeth wicked devices to pass. (Psalm 37:1–7)

Most people grow up believing that if they do well in school, work hard, and are generally a nice person, everything will turn out all right in their lives. The world tells us to trust in our education, occupations, relationships, physical health, and in our country for well-being. In reality, this is the weakest form of trust you can have. Everything we see and experience in the natural during this lifetime is subject to change. And it will change.

Why do we insist on trusting only what we can see and touch? I believe it is because we do not know what it truly means to trust. We do not know how to trust in the Lord fully. There is a trust that is a secret place, a place of pure love and peace, and you can go to be with Him there.

Psalm 91:1–2 says, "He that dwelleth in the secret place of the most high shall abide under the shadow of the Almighty. I will say of the Lord, he is my refuge and my fortress: my God; in him will I trust."

When you go to the Lord in times of prayer, worship, praise, or study, you are building a relationship with almighty God so that He becomes your sustenance. He *is* the secret place, and with Him it becomes clear that God is more real than whatever your needs are. He becomes your answer to anything and everything. God is your daddy, husband, friend, mother, sister, provider, healer, teacher, and counselor. He is the only answer that will fully satisfy and solve all life's needs and trials. The more you know His nature, the more soundly His truth will reign in your heart.

However, that does not mean you won't get hurt in life. You will be hurt by people, go through hardships in your finances, and get sick in your body. If you think you are going to serve the Lord and not get hurt, that is not true. What that kind of thinking is, is a fairy tale, and oh, how Satan loves fairy tales! If he can get you to believe a fairy tale, it will not take much to get you off your horse and out of the race.

Satan's fairy tale can amend to anyone's life: Grow up, fall in love, have children, and live happily ever after. Grow up, fall in love, get saved, have children, and live happily ever after. Grow up, fall in love, get a college degree, make a lot of money, get saved, have children, and live happily ever after. Need I go on?

I'm sure one of those hit you too. Why? Because Satan uses the same lies on all of us over and over again. These lies are fairy tales we have bit into, and they all leave us wounded, discouraged, and tired.

The truth is that people will get hurt by people, people will get sick, and people will go through times of hardship financially even though we are saved. Why? Because of the fall of humankind in the Garden of Gethsemane in Genesis. The curse was imparted at that time. We have been redeemed from the curse of the law as Galatians 3:13 says, "Christ hath redeemed us from the curse of the Law by becoming a curse for us. For it is written: 'Cursed is everyone who is hung on a tree.' However, the curse is still here and because of lack of knowledge we fall into the ways of the curse that still exists here. The Word says this, 'My people are destroyed for lack of knowledge …'" (Hosea 4:6).

Through salvation we have been redeemed from the curse of the law, but it is still here. This is why you must trust the Lord; this is why there is a secret place made for you and me. A place of peace, comfort, joy, love, health, and all that is good. It is meant to keep Satan and his band of followers out. It is a place where you can live in the turmoil of this world with a stance of gladness.

The Word of God in its entirety teaches you how to lean in and trust in God's plan for your future; how to trust when you are in trouble, trust in hope, trust in faith and love, trust in endurance and patience.

There isn't a scenario in life that it will not cover. His Word is deep and wide with revelation. It is Him. And when you get hold of this revelation through the Holy Spirit, you will see with your heart and know that you are now in that secret place. Only the ones who go in with the Holy Spirit and meditate in His Word with a seeking humble heart to worship His majesty may enter.

The Words says this about trust:

> Have I not commanded you? Be strong and courageous. Do not be terrified; do not be discouraged, for the Lord your God will be with you wherever you go. (Joshua 1:9 AMP)

Those who know your name will trust in you, for you, Lord, have never forsaken those who seek you. (Psalm 9:10 NIV)

But I trust in your unfailing love; my heart rejoices in your salvation. (Psalm 13:5 NIV)

Some trust in chariots and some in horses, but we trust in the name of the Lord our God. (Psalm 20:7 NIV)

But I trust in you, O Lord; I say, "You are my God." (Psalm 31:14 NIV)

When I am afraid, I will trust in you. (Psalm 56:3 NKJ)

Lord Almighty, blessed is the man who trusts in you. (Psalm 84:12 NIV)

Trust in the Lord with all your heart and lean not on your own understanding; in all your ways acknowledge him, and he will make your paths straight. (Proverbs 3:5–6 NIV)

But now, this is what the Lord, your Creator says, says, Jacob, And He who formed you, O Israel, Do not fear, "Fear not, for I have redeemed you(from captivity);I have called you by name; you are Mine! (Isaiah 43:1 AMP)

The king was overjoyed and gave orders to lift Daniel out of the den. And when Daniel was lifted from the den, no wound was found on him, because he had trusted in his God. (Daniel 6:23 NIV)

Do not let your hearts be troubled. Trust in God; trust also in me. (John 14:1 NLT)

May the God of hope fill you with all joy and peace as you trust in him, so that you may overflow with hope by the power of the Holy Spirit. (Romans 15:13 NIV)

He who was seated on the throne said, "I am making everything new!" Then he said, "Write this down, for these words are trustworthy and true." (Revelation 21:5 NIV)

The God of my rock; in him will I trust: he is my shield, and the horn of my salvation, my high tower, and my refuge, my savior; thou savest me from violence. (2 Samuel 22:3)

Start today. Find a place daily to read, pray, worship, and study His Word. It will lead you into the secret place. To those who knock, it shall be opened.

Matthew 7:7–8 says, "Ask, and it shall be given; Seek ye shall find; Knock, and it shall be opened unto you. For everyone that asketh receiveth; and he that seeketh findeth; and to him that knocketh it shall be opened."

Fret not, and follow the voice of your Shepherd into the secret place of the Most High God. It is only there you will be satisfied with your life, in your life, for the rest of your life.

6

YOU MUST BE OCCUPIED

YEARS AGO, THE Holy Spirit spoke something to my spirit. My daughter was a junior in high school, and she rode the school bus home every day. She would walk through the door singing songs she heard on the bus. I tried to tell her that the music she was singing was not godly. I wanted my daughter to have good influences in her life. And of course she disagreed with me that the music was a negative influence. We went round and round, arguing about it for two weeks.

One day I was walking through our kitchen to go out to the garage. There was a place on the way out that I was always trying to keep free from clutter. As I walked out the kitchen door, I wondered, *Why can't I keep that spot empty?*

Immediately the Holy Spirit said, "All empty space must be occupied."

I knew in that moment that He was talking about my daughter. The Lord was showing me that He established a law in the beginning when He said, "be fruitful, and multiply, and replenish the earth" (Genesis 1:28 ASV).

He created us with physical and emotional needs, needs that will be fulfilled either by His love or by earthly means. Just as we can choose to fill our stomachs with good food or junk food, we can either fill our minds with God's Word or the world's teaching. And we were created with a love for music.

The Lord told me, "You can't stop her from hearing what is being played on the radio on that bus or from singing it afterwards." He said, "Put her tape recorder on the kitchen counter, and put her favorite Christian tape in. When she gets home, turn it on so that it is playing when she walks in."

I did as He said. The next day my daughter walked in through the kitchen, right by the song that was playing, and into her bedroom to drop off her backpack. She came out of the bedroom, and within minutes, she was singing the song that was playing on the countertop. I never had to say anther word again. God is so good.

She was singing the music from the school bus because it was what she heard. It occupied the place within her that craves music. When we hear good music, we automatically enjoy it and desire to be filled with that sound. When my daughter heard the Christian music, it pushed the last song out and embraced the new one.

This is powerful information: Every place in your being *will be occupied*. We are created for love, peace, joy, security, and the fruits of the Spirit. It is amazing how easily these desires for nourishment can be filled with hate, fear, depression, jealousy, and more. It is your choice!

7

YOUR PLACES

WHEN YOU FELLOWSHIP with the Lord daily, He will begin to occupy the places you open up to Him. The more of yourself you make available to the Lord, the more He will fill you with His Word, truly satisfying your needs such as love, peace, healing, blessing, and wisdom. He will give you peace where you once held fear. He will be a counselor in one area of your life and a healer in another. His presence will become as real to you as someone sitting next to you.

Do you see it? As you allow the Lord to fulfill a need in your life, the complete satisfaction of His presence will draw you to invite Him into other areas within you.

I remember talking with my brother Steve about the Lord, and he shared a thought with me. He said that the reason people get addicted to drugs, alcohol, and many other things is that we were created to be addicted to the presence of God. I could not agree more.

"Addicted" means, "Dependent: Very enthusiastic: Very interested in a particular thing and devoting a lot of time to it" (*Merriam-Webster Online*).

As we spend time with God, we invite Him into every place in our lives. We become dependent on Him. We become addicted to His presence.

Oh, the precious fruit that you bear when you are that close to the

Lord. It is life! Do you know what life means? I think we tend to believe that life is defined by breath, but a person can be breathing while a dead man's bones are walking. Matthew 23:27 says, "Woe unto you, scribes and Pharisees, hypocrites! For ye are like unto whited sepulchers, which indeed appear beautiful outward, but are within full of dead men's bones, and of all uncleanness."

People all over the world are talking, walking, and breathing, but they are filled with hatred, envy, idolatry, wrath, strife, drunkenness, and more. Life, however, is filled with love, joy, peace, longsuffering, gentleness, goodness, faith, meekness, and temperance (Galatians 5:19–23). It is the fruit of the spirit.

John 1:4 says, "In him was life; and the life was the light of men."

And in Genesis 2:9, the Bible says, "out of the ground made the Lord God to grow every tree that is pleasant to the sight, and good for food; the tree of *life* also in the midst of the garden, and the tree of knowledge of good and evil" (emphasis mine).

In Luke 6:43, Jesus says,

> For a good tree bringeth not forth corrupt fruit; neither doth a corrupt tree bring forth good fruit. For every tree is known by his own fruit. For of thorns men do not gather figs, nor of a bramble bush gather they grapes. A good man out of the good treasure of his heart bringeth forth that which is good; and an evil man out of the evil treasure of his heart bringeth forth that, which is evil: for of the abundance of the heart his mouth speaketh.

What you allow yourself to be filled with will determine your outcome.

8

TREES THAT WE EAT

GENESIS TELLS US that there are two trees from which we can eat: the Tree of Life and the Tree of the Knowledge of Good and Evil. You will eat from one, the other, or both. The latter will cause you to become a dead man's bones walking. If you eat from both trees, then your life will bear a mixture of sweet and bitter fruit. But allowing the Lord to inhabit every area of your life will produce the fruit of life!

This life is an incredible journey. What an honor that God Almighty, the Creator of heaven and earth, cares about *everything* we go through. Eating from the Tree of Life means spending time with the Lord, listening to His voice, following His Word, letting Him lead you through life's journey, surrendering to His way, and being filled with the fruit of the Spirit. That is not a cliché; it is real! Your life's fruit will be evident in what you accomplish and, most important, how you affect other people.

Eating from the other tree will fill you, but you will be filled with the fruit of death. Being a Christian means salvation from hell, but becoming a Christian is *far* from the last choice a believer makes. The life that has been given to us must be sought after. You must pursue the Lord in every area of your life to experience fully the great gift that Jesus died to give us. John 17:16 says that "We live in this world, but we are not of the world." It is possible to be full of the Holy Spirit in one area of your life, while another area is still being fed from the Tree of the Knowledge of Good and Evil.

The death of this fruit shows up in our lives in the forms of fear, addiction, anxiety, lack, sorrow, depression, tiredness, doubt, gluttony, and more. And the lord of that tree is Satan. He seeks to fill as many areas of your life with this fruit as you allow. He cannot keep you from salvation, but he can deceive you and keep you from receiving your full blessing and walking in authority as a son of God. Satan wants to come in through the mind so that he can thwart God's plan for your life and destroy you. He wants to keep you from the secret place and from knowing your Creator, who loves you and will do anything for you when you ask. John 14:14 says, "If ye ask anything in my name, I will do it."

Satan does not want you to spend any time with Jesus because he knows that he will lose ground. God is God to many people, but when He becomes their Lord, He is given authority in their lives to accomplish His good purpose on the earth. The devil hates and fears that. He hates God, and he hates you. He is bitter, jealous, and miserable. His destiny is hell! He has no second chance and no future life. That makes him dangerous because he has nothing to lose, and he will go to every length to deceive humankind.

My heart longs to see people trust, rely on, and press into the safety of God's presence. I hurt to see so many people struggling when Jesus paid such a high price for them to have peace.

Hebrews 4:15 says, "For we have not a high priest which cannot be touched with the feeling of our infirmities; but was in all points tempted like as we are, yet without sin."

He went through every temptation and trial that you will ever face. Why? So He could return to the Father as the perfect High Priest. One who will intercede for you, a mediator for God and His children.

Jesus longs to commune with His people. He has given everything to you, but instead of you receiving it, He watches many people live lives apart from Him, eating from the wrong tree, building their lives upon lies, which is sinking sand.

Humans walked away from their own blessing because the god of this world blinded their minds.

You might say, "I want to have this life that you have been talking about. But how? I always end up right back where I started."

That is because you are trying to accomplish God's good work through your own power. We cannot do anything on our own. Remember: humans were separated from God in the beginning and left helpless. Once you have asked Jesus to come into your heart, give Him all your life. Then ask the Holy Spirit to fill you, and you will be filled with His power too.

> For God hath not given us the spirit of fear; but of *power,*
> love and a sound mind." (2 Timothy 1:7; emphasis mine).

Let's take a look at the word "power." "Power" means, "capacity to do something: the ability, strength, and capacity to do something" (*Dictionary.com*).

> And, behold, I send the promise of my Father upon you: but tarry ye in the city of Jerusalem, until ye be endued with *power* from on high. (Luke 24:49; emphasis mine)

> But ye shall receive *power,* after that the Holy Ghost is come upon you: and ye shall be witnessed unto me both in Jerusalem, and in all Judea, and in Samaria, and unto the uttermost part of the earth. (Acts 1:8; emphasis mine)

> And they were all *filled* with the Holy Ghost, and began to speak with other tongues, as the Spirit gave them utterance. (Acts 2:4; emphasis mine)

> And when they had set them in the midst, they asked, By what power, or by what name, have ye done this? Then Peter *filled* with the Holy Ghost, said unto them, Ye rulers of the people, and elders of Israel. (Acts 4:7–8; emphasis mine)

> And when they had prayed, the place was shaken where they were assembled together; and they were all *filled* with

the Holy Ghost, and they spake the word of God with *boldness*. (Acts 4:31; emphasis mine)

Then Saul (who also is called Paul) *filled* with the Holy Ghost, set his eyes on him. (Acts 13:9; emphasis mine)

These men could do nothing before Jesus left. They walked with Him for three years, and their discernment was unborn. Their faith was parked in what they could reason with in their minds. And as far as power and boldness, they all eventually walked away from the ministry that Jesus told them to follow until He showed Himself alive after His death, before His ascension to the Father!

The same is true for you and me before we invite Christ to fill our lives. The glorious reality is that you and I can have power and strength to overcome everything. There is nothing you cannot overcome! God's Word says that we can do *all* things through Christ who strengthens us (Philippians 4:13).

God gave everything to make a way for us—the way of the kingdom of Heaven. He gave His life for us, and He plants His life in us. God wants to be involved in everything you do. He wants you to conquer the trials in your life. He wants you to be healthy and prosperous. He wants you to walk in His glory for His name's sake (Psalm 106:8). All His power resides within you; that was God's master plan back in the Garden of Eden. When Satan stole His children—the love and joy of His life—God had a plan, and there was nothing Satan and his demons could do to thwart it. Hallelujah!

Jesus came to earth, died for us, and before He left said:

> Go ye into all the world, and preach the gospel to every creature. He that believeth and is baptized shall be saved; but he that believeth not shall be damned. And these signs shall follow them that believe; In my name shall they cast out devils; they shall speak with new tongues; They shall take up serpents; and if they drink any deadly thing, it shall not hurt them; they shall lay hands on the sick, and they shall recover. (Mark 16:15–18)

And then in His faithfulness, God sent His promise, the Holy Spirit, so that when we are saved, we can be filled with His power, His love, and His purpose!

Jesus prophesied about the Holy Spirit, saying, "And I will pray to the Father, and he shall give you another Comforter, that he may abide with you forever; Even the spirit of truth; whom the world cannot receive, because it seeth him not, you neither knoweth him: but the living God dwells within us, and you know him; for He dwelleth with you, and shall be *in* you" (John 14:16; emphasis mine).

All we have to do is make room for Him to occupy every area of our life. He will become the stronger one in us. The Word says, "Greater is he that is in us than he that is in the world" (1 John 4:4). That is a glorious possibility but not an automatic reality. God will not be the greater *in you* if you do not *allow* Him to be.

You cannot afford to cling to your own ways. In Him, the power you will have in your own life will be amazing. In Him, your mind and emotions will be under your dominion, not the other way around. Aren't you fed up with the same old stuff in your life? Let it go today. Right now! Tell the Father that you want Him to lead in every area of your life.

Start developing your relationship with Christ today. Do not wait. He is right there waiting for you. Confess to the Holy Spirit that you need His help. Talk to Him like a trustworthy friend. He is your helper. He is your teacher. He is on the earth for you! He is just waiting for people to let Him in.

The Word says, "For the eyes of the Lord run to and fro throughout the earth, to shew himself strong in the behalf of them whose heart is perfect toward him. Herein thou hast done foolishly: therefore, from henceforth thou shalt have wars" (2 Chronicles 16:9).

I said earlier that you will give each place in your life over to something. The choice is either to trust in the truth that God will lead you into a better life than you can, or to believe the enemy's lie that you can satisfy your own needs with things of this world. Do not give the old serpent any part of your blood-bought life. Stand in the kingdom of God and say to the devil, "No more will I let you steal my blessing!"

Ephesians 1:3 says, "blessed be the God and Father of our Lord Jesus

Christ, who hath blessed us with all spiritual blessings in heavenly places in Christ."

When you stand up for the men and women serving in the military and say, "I support you and thank you for what you are doing for our country," you bring honor to them. In the same way, you bring honor to Jesus when you stand on His Word and say, "By His stripes, I am healed." Your words testify to your belief in what He did for you, and you are thanking Him as well as receiving His truth in your life. I, for one, want to honor my Lord, my love, and my life.

9

SEPARATED

I TALK TO a lot of people in my line of work. I remember talking with one woman in particular a few years ago. She shared something with me that I had never thought about, but after she said it, I knew it had to be so.

She said, "You know, I believe Jesus was lonely at times. I mean here He was on earth, and there was no one to sit down and fellowship with. There wasn't anyone on His level of spiritual knowledge. He had no one to sit around with and talk about the things of God."

I thought about that conversation for a long time afterwards, and I knew it was true. When you get around people who have no clue about the Lord, salvation, baptism of the Holy Spirit, you miss talking about the great things of God. You feel lonely. Separated. Well Jesus was always teaching, healing, and praying for others. He desired someone to understand what He was teaching so that He could relate with them on His level.

Jesus said, "O ye of little faith, why reason ye among your selves, because ye have brought no bread? Do ye not understand ... How is it that ye do not understand that I spake it not to you concerning bread" (Matthew 16:8–9, 11). He was frustrated with His disciples because they did not understand what he was teaching. He traveled, ate, drank, and prayed with his disciples, and as he taught, he could see they still were looking at him with blank stares.

How frustrating that must have been. That would be like you living in your home, and your family did not have a clue about your ways of love, care, and intentions you had for them, when what you desire is for them to embrace your intimate thoughts toward them.

Worse yet, He was about to go through the most agonizing trial any human being would ever experience. No one was there to pray for Him or with Him. He had no one to encourage Him in His great trial. He went through it alone.

In the Garden of Gethsemane, He left his disciples and asked them to watch with Him while he prayed. When He returned the first, second, and third times, they were asleep. Jesus confronted His calling alone.

Do you feel like you are alone and no one understands you or your sacrifice you are about to give or are already giving? You are not alone. Jesus sees you, and He has walked this road before you. Allow the Holy Spirit to guide you through your life as He guided Jesus while He lived on earth. It is there that you can do all things through Christ who strengthens you (Philippians 4:13).

You are not alone; you have almighty God residing within you. He will fill every ounce of your being with His presence if you allow him to.

He is the great I Am, Alpha and Omega, the Prince of Peace, healer, deliverer. He is all!

Move forward with Him. He will fill your life with excitement, and your destiny will come to pass. Yes, your journey will be one to pray through, to fight for at times. But the ramifications of not pursuing your life's call is one of dry times, depressed times, living with no purpose. And that is a place I never ever want to be.

Draw to your Lord and Savior, and become one with Him. He desires your intimacy.

10

COMMUNION

WHAT DOES COMMUNION mean?

Merriam-Webster Online defines "communion" as, "Intimacy: a feeling of emotional or spiritual closeness" or, "Connection: a relationship, especially one in which something is communicated or shared."

Jesus wanted to share the Passover meal with His disciples. He desired spiritual closeness with them. He desired connection and understanding. "I am the vine, ye are the branches," He said. "He that abideth in me and I in him, the same bringeth forth much fruit for without me ye can do nothing. If ye abide in me, and my words abide in you, ye shall ask what ye will and it shall be done unto you" (John 15: 5, 7). He desired fellowship.

> Greater love hath no man than this, that ye love one another, as I have loved you. Ye are my friends, if ye do whatsoever I command you. Henceforth I call you not servants; for the servant knoweth not what his Lord doeth: but I have called you friends; for all things that I have heard of my Father I have made known unto you. (John 15:13–15)

Jesus wants us to be His closest friends. He desires a close relationship with *you*! And He is waiting for you to enter into His presence. He gave His life for you and called you His friend.

When Jesus shared the Passover with His disciples, the bread He lifted was a symbol of His flesh, representing what He was about to do. Luke 22:19 says, "And he took bread, and gave thanks, and brake it, and gave unto them, saying, 'This is my body which is given for you: this do in remembrance of me. This cup is the new testament in my blood, which is shed for you.'"

Christ's own body is the most intimate thing He could share with someone, and He chose to share it with you. He shared His life, His death, His resurrection. His glorious future can be your glorious future. You did nothing to deserve it; you did not earn it. It is a gift from God.

Jesus rewrote the covenant for you. He rewrote the covenant in His blood. Remember often the life He lived. He used his power boldly. He laid hands on the sick and healed them. He cast out demons to free the oppressed. He commanded storms to stop, and the sky obeyed. He cursed trees, and they dried up from the roots. Now He is asking us to remember what He did, take on His name, and do the same.

Jesus will give His name and inheritance to you so that you can walk through your life on this earth with power, strength, and ability. Remember Him! He has restored your authority by dying for you, shedding His blood for you. He paid your price.

> And he said unto them, Go Ye (Ye, means You!) into all the world, and preach the gospel to every creature. He that believeth and is baptized shall be saved; but he that believeth not shall be damned. And these signs shall follow them that believe; In *my name* shall they cast out devils; they shall speak with new tongues; Thou shall take up serpents; and if they drink any deadly thing, it shall not hurt them; they shall lay hands on the sick, and they shall recover. (Mark 16:15–20; emphasis mine)

All power is given unto me in heaven and in earth. Go ye therefore, and teach all nations, baptizing them in the name of the father, and of the Son, and of the Holy Ghost: Teaching them to observe all things whatsoever I have *commanded* you: and, lo I am with you always, even unto the end of the world. (Matthew 28:18; emphasis mine)

11

HEALING

SURELY, HE HATH borne our griefs and carried our sorrows: yet we did esteem him stricken, smitten of God, and afflicted. But He was wounded for our transgressions; He was bruised for our iniquities: the chastisement of our peace was upon him; and with His stripes we are healed. (Isaiah 53:4–5)

> Christ hath redeemed us from the curse of the law, being made a curse *for us*: for it is written, cursed is everyone that hangeth on a tree: That the blessing of Abraham might come on the Gentiles through faith. (Galatians 3:13; emphasis mine)

Jesus, the Lord of creation, was obedient to death. As He ate His last meal with His disciples, He was preparing to die. That sacred meal set the tone of God's plan.

First Corinthians 2:7–8 says, "But we speak of the wisdom of God in a mystery, even the hidden wisdom, which God ordained before the world of glory. Which *none* of the *princes* knew: for hath they known it, they would not have crucified the Lord of glory" (emphasis mine).

Jesus was about to dot the i's and cross the ts on the new covenant. Satan had no idea the mastery God had hidden in Jesus. He went to the cross bearing the sins of the world on His flesh and in His spirit. He received the punishment for all the disobedience of humankind. He bore the chastisement, all the rebuke of the Father. He bore the iniquity of humankind, the great injustice, extreme immorality on His flesh. He took every grief and sorrow upon Himself. And by His stripes, we are healed.

Then He went to hell and took the keys of death from Satan while the ranks of His demons watched. He defeated the god of this world on his territory. Then Jesus rose from the dead, and when He rose, He gave all power and authority right back to humans, as it was in the beginning.

It was a checkmate! It was touché! It was I win; you lose! Forever!

Just as before, Satan lost. He believed he had the world in his hand for all eternity, but in an instant, as it seemed, he was back on the sidelines looking in, just as he was in the Garden of Eden. However, this time he still has a short time on this earth before he is cast into the eternal lake of fire.

> And the beast was taken, and with him the false prophet
> that wrought miracles before him, with which he deceived
> them that had received the mark of the beast, and them
> that worshipped his image. These both were cast alive into
> a lake of fire burning with brimstone. (Revelation 19:20)

There are many people who do not know the truth of God's Word. Satan reigns on earth causing sickness, disease, catastrophic natural events, wars, poverty, starvation, and death. He is ranting and raving about his evil plans and operating without a license. But you have the license, and that license is Jesus's name. Satan has no choice but to leave his place as you command by the authority Christ gave you.

The devil is not a new revelation on the earth. He was in the Garden of Eden when it all began, and he is here now. It is our charge to handle him once and for all, the same way Adam and Eve should have. Do not listen to him; he is a liar, and his words cannot stand up to God's Word, which is truth.

Jesus went to heaven and sent the Holy Spirit, the comforter, to live within you so that you can live and walk in the same authority and peace He experienced. The same Spirit that lived in Him now lives in you!

Romans 8:11 says, "But if the Spirit of him that raised up Jesus from the dead dwell in you, he that raised up Christ from the dead shall also quicken your mortal bodies by his Spirit that dwelleth in you."

And you can live without fear, sickness and poverty because the curse has been defeated. According to Galatians 3:13, "Christ hath redeemed us from the curse of the law, being made a curse for us: for it is written, Cursed is everyone that hangeth on a tree."

Glory be to God! Jesus is Lord!

How are you going to live out your remaining days? Are you going to allow Satan to use your mind and emotions to accomplish his purpose on the earth, or will you allow God—your Father—to spread His glory through you on the earth?

It's your choice!

SALVATION PRAYER

Father, I repent of my sins. I ask Jesus to come into my heart and be Lord over my life. I ask that You use my life for Your glory. Thank You.

REFERENCES

Amplified Bible-Online.

King James Bible-Online.

Merriam-Webster Online Dictionary

New International Version Bible-Online.

New King James Bible-Online.

New Living Testament-Online.

Wikipedia.

04090120-00836569

Printed in the United States
by Baker & Taylor Publisher Services